SPACE TOOLS

David and Patricia Armentrout

A Crabtree Seedlings Book

Table of Contents

Exploring Space 4
Telescopes 6
Rockets 11
The International Space Station 14
Space Probes 18
Rovers 20
Glossary 23
Index 23

Exploring Space

Long ago, **astronomers** had only their eyes and a few ancient tools to help them learn about space. Still, they identified many objects in our **solar system**.

Galileo was first to use a telescope to study space.

Galileo Galilei
1564 – 1642

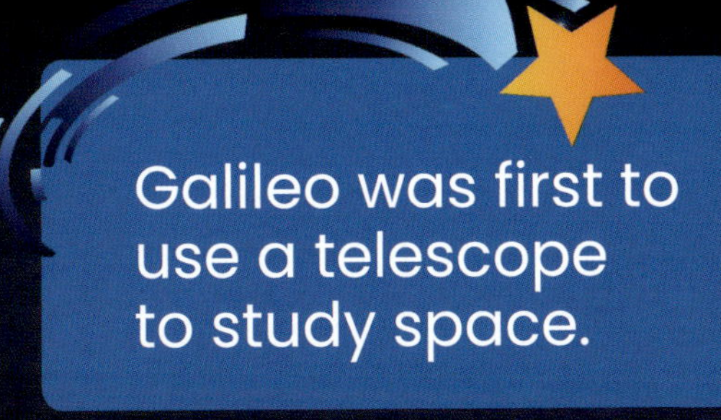

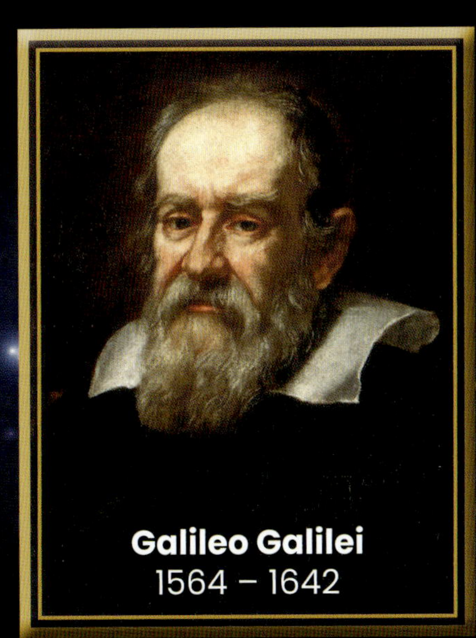

Saturn
Neptune
Uranus
Jupiter

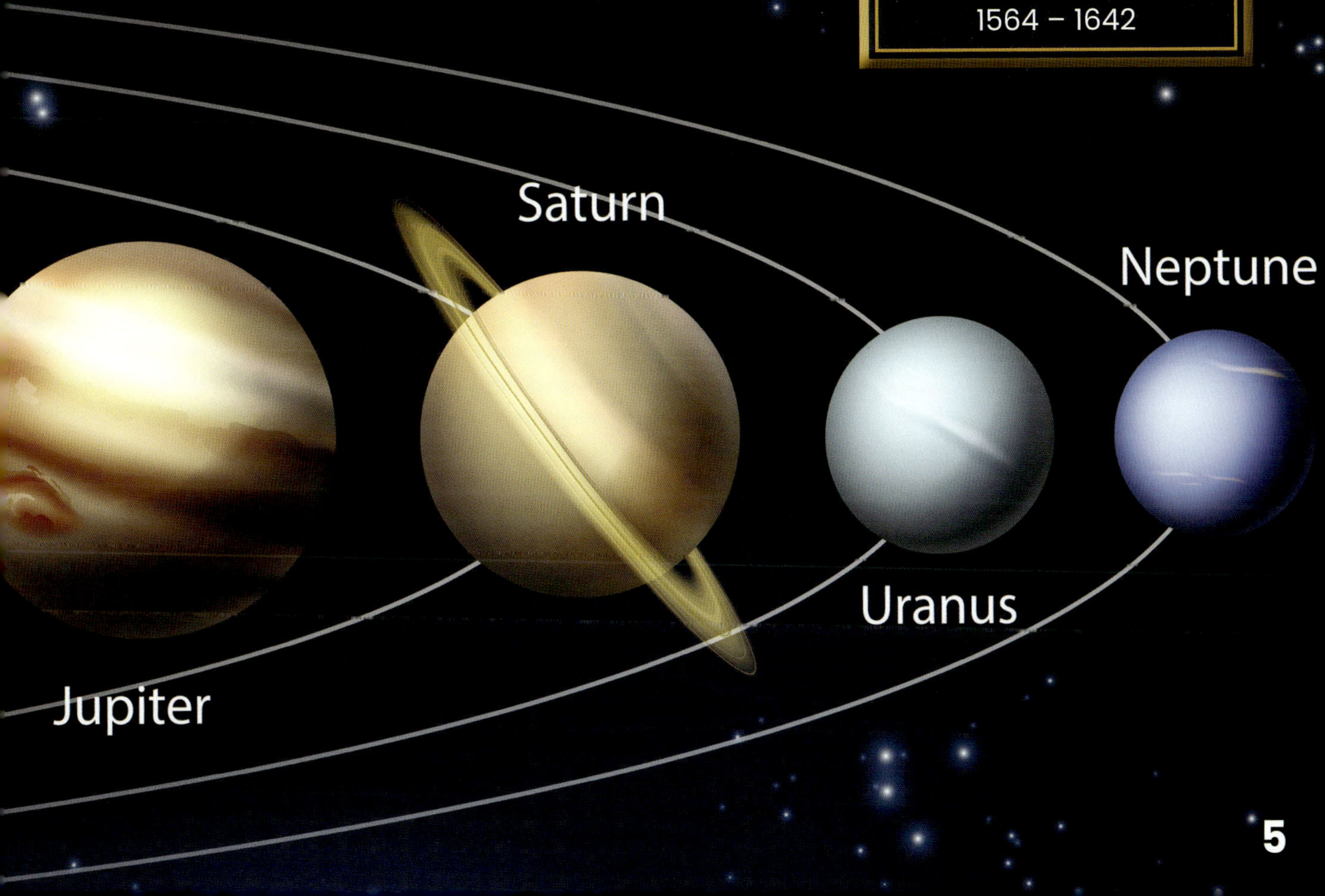

Telescopes

Telescopes are tools that make distant objects appear closer. The first telescopes produced blurry images.

The Mauna Kea **Observatories**, in Hawaii, have some of the world's largest optical telescopes. These are telescopes that gather light to show an image.

Despite that, telescopes helped astronomers take the next step in space exploration.

The Hubble Space Telescope may be the most famous telescope. It takes pictures of our solar system and deep space as it **orbits** Earth.

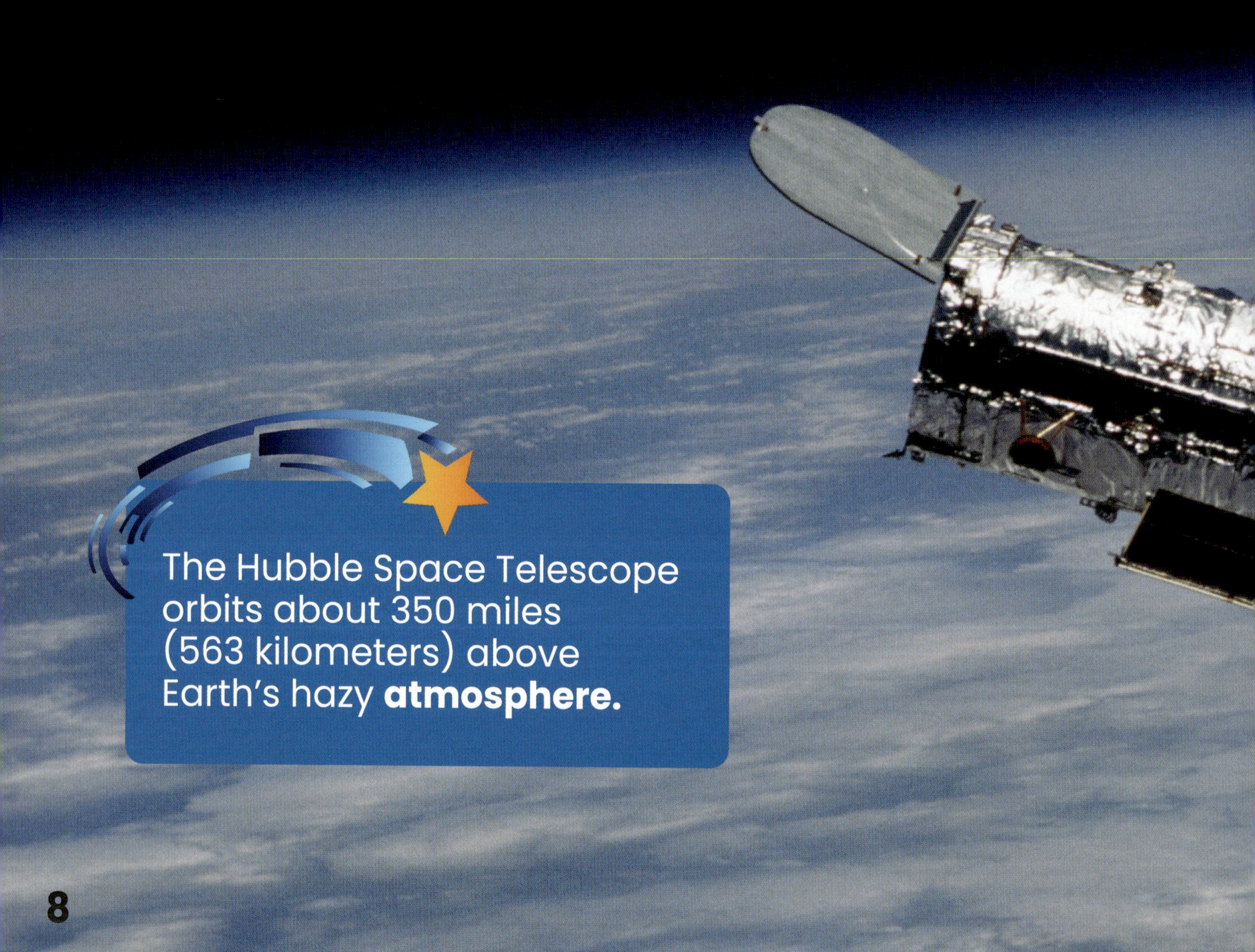

The Hubble Space Telescope orbits about 350 miles (563 kilometers) above Earth's hazy **atmosphere.**

Astronauts have made several repairs to the Hubble Space Telescope in space.

The James Webb Space Telescope (JWST) is NASA's next generation space-based telescope. It will use new **technology** to peer deeper into space.

The JWST will not orbit Earth like the Hubble Space Telescope. Instead, it will orbit the Sun, 932,057 miles (500,000 kilometers) from Earth.

NASA stands for National Aeronautics and Space Administration.

Rockets

Five, four, three, two, one. Lift off! A count down happens just before a rocket launches into space. Rockets are important space tools.

Rockets are used to launch satellites, space telescopes, and other spacecraft.

The two-stage *Falcon 9* launch vehicle lifts off from Cape Canaveral Air Force Station, in Florida. It carries the *Dragon* resupply spacecraft to the International Space Station.

Objects that orbit Earth are called satellites. Hundreds of human-made satellites orbit Earth.

The SpaceX *Dragon* resupply spacecraft separates from the *Falcon 9* rocket when it arrives in orbit. It then uses solar arrays for power.

The SpaceX *Dragon* resupply spacecraft delivers supplies, equipment, and experiments to the International Space Station.

The International Space Station

The International Space Station (ISS) is a space laboratory. The ISS was not built on Earth, then launched into space. It would have been too large and too heavy. It was taken into space piece by piece.

The ISS is slightly larger than an American football field.

The ISS has been gradually built in space by astronauts.

The ISS has more than an acre (0.4 hectares) of solar arrays.
This makes it the second brightest object in the night sky, after the Moon.

Astronauts live aboard the ISS, usually for months at a time. There, they conduct experiments and gather information. Scientists use the information to plan future missions.

Scientists are studying plants in space. When astronauts start traveling farther into space, they will need to grow plants in space for food. Plants can also be a valuable source of oxygen.

Space Probes

A space probe is a robot that collects information. The *Voyager 1* probe was launched in 1977. Its mission was to explore the solar system. *Voyager 1* has now gone beyond our solar system.

NASA has sent space probes to every planet in our solar system.

Voyager 1

It is farther from Earth than any other human-made object. It is still operating as it flies deeper into space.

Rovers

Rovers are space vehicles. During the *Apollo* Moon missions, astronauts drove rovers as they explored the Moon's surface.

Lunar Roving Vehicle, *Apollo 17* mission

NASA's Mars rover, *Curiosity*, is remote controlled. Its mission is to discover whether Mars was ever able to support life.

Commands are sent to *Curiosity* using NASA's Deep Space Network.

Another NASA rover, *Perseverance*, has new and improved science tools to explore Mars further than ever before.

People still stare up at the stars. We all wonder about our place in the solar system.

Glossary

astronauts (AS-struh-nawts): People trained for space flight.

astronomers (uh-STRON-uh-merz): People who study objects in space.

atmosphere (AT-muhss-fihr): A layer of gases around a planet.

observatories (uhb-ZUR-vuh-tor-eez): Buildings containing telescopes and other science instruments.

orbits (OR-bits): Travels in an invisible path around a larger object like a planet or star.

solar system (SOH-lur SIS-tuhm): A star and all the planets and space objects that travel around it.

technology (TEK-nahl-uh-jee): The use of science knowledge to invent useful things.

Index

International Space Station (ISS) 12, 13, 14, 15, 16
probe 18
rockets 11, 12, 13
rover(s) 20, 21, 22
satellites 12
solar system 4, 8, 18, 22
telescope(s) 5, 6, 7, 8, 10, 12

School-to-Home Support for Caregivers and Teachers

This book helps children grow by letting them practice reading. Here are a few guiding questions to help the reader build his or her comprehension skills. Possible answers appear here in red.

Before Reading

- **What do I think this book is about?** I think this book is about the tools that are used to study space. I think this book is about telescopes.
- **What do I want to learn about this topic?** I want to learn how telescopes are made. I want to learn how to become an astronaut.

During Reading

- **I wonder why...** I wonder why NASA chose to have a space telescope orbit the Sun. I wonder why rockets are sent into space.
- **What have I learned so far?** I have learned that the International Space Station was built in space. I have learned that scientists are studying plants in space so that future astronauts can grow their own food in space.

After Reading

- **What details did I learn about this topic?** I have learned that rovers are space vehicles. I have learned that some rovers are driven by astronauts and others are remote controlled.
- **Read the book again and look for the glossary words.** I see the word ***observatories*** on page 6, and the word ***orbits*** on page 8. The other glossary words are found on page 23.

Library and Archives Canada Cataloguing in Publication

CIP available at Library and Archives Canada

Library of Congress Cataloging-in-Publication Data

CIP available at Library of Congress

Crabtree Publishing Company
www.crabtreebooks.com 1–800–387–7650

Print book version produced jointly with Blue Door Education in 2022

PHOTO CREDITS:
Cover courtesy of NASA; pages 4-5 By Christos Georghiou / Shutterstock.com; pages 6-7 observatory By Semisatch / Shutterstock.com; hubble telescope pages 8, 9, 10 courtesy of NASA; page 11 NASA/Bill Ingalls; page 16 © 3Dsculptor | Shutterstock.com, page 12-17 courtesy of NASA; page 18-19 NASA/JPL-Caltech; page 20 and 22 NASA; page 21 NASA/JPL-Caltech/MSSS

Written by: David and Patricia Armentrout
Production coordinator and Prepress technician: Tammy McGarr
Print coordinator: Katherine Berti

Printed in the U.S.A./CG20210915/012022

Published in the United States
Crabtree Publishing
347 Fifth Ave.
Suite 1402-145
New York, NY 10016

Published in Canada
Crabtree Publishing
616 Welland Ave.
St. Catharines, Ontario
L2M 5V6